SOJOURNER TRUTH'S "AIN'T I A WOMAN?"

FRONT SEAT OF HISTORY: FAMOUS SPEECHES

TAMRA ORR

CHERRY LAKE PRESS

Published in the United States of America by Cherry Lake Publishing Group
Ann Arbor, Michigan
www.cherrylakepublishing.com

Reading Adviser: Marla Conn, MS, Ed., Literacy specialist, Read-Ability, Inc.
Content Adviser: Adam Fulton Johnson, PhD, Assistant Professor, History, Philosophy, and Sociology of Science, Michigan State University
Photo credits: © Alpha Historica/Alamy Stock Photo, cover; © Library of Congress, LC-DIG-ppmsca-52069, 5; © Everett Historical/Shutterstock.com, 6, 8, 9, 10, 14, 28 [top], 28 [bottom], 29 [top]; © Library of Congress, LC-USZ62-16225, 13; © Glasshouse Images/Alamy Stock Photo, 16; © Universal Images Group North America LLC/Alamy Stock Photo, 19; © NATNN/Shutterstock.com, 20; © Library of Congress, LC-DIG-ds-13262, 23; © U.S. Information Agency, U.S. National Archives, 24; © U.S. National Archives, 111-SC-162466, 25; © Diego G Diaz/Shutterstock.com, 26; © Keith Lance/ iStock.com, 29 [bottom]

Cherry Lake Press is an imprint of Cherry Lake Publishing Group.

Library of Congress Cataloging-in-Publication Data
Names: Orr, Tamra, author.
Title: Sojourner Truth's "Ain't I a woman?" / by Tamra Orr.
Description: Ann Arbor, Michigan : Cherry Lake Publishing, 2021 | Series: Front seat of history: famous speeches | Includes index. | Audience: Grades 4-6
Identifiers: LCCN 2020005753 (print) | LCCN 2020005754 (ebook) | ISBN 9781534168763 (hardcover) | ISBN 9781534170445 (paperback) | ISBN 9781534172289 (pdf) | ISBN 9781534174122 (ebook)
Subjects: LCSH: Truth, Sojourner, 1799-1883—Juvenile literature. | African American abolitionists—Biography—Juvenile literature. | Abolitionists—United States—Biography—Juvenile literature. | African American women—Biography—Juvenile literature. | Social reformers—United States—Biography—Juvenile literature. | Truth, Sojourner, 1799-1883—Oratory—Juvenile literature. | Speeches, addresses, etc., American—African American authors—History and criticism—Juvenile literature. | Speeches, addresses, etc., American—Women authors—History and criticism—Juvenile literature. | African American women—Intellectual life—Juvenile literature. | Women and literature—United States—Juvenile literature.
Classification: LCC E185.97.T8 O77 2021 (print) | LCC E185.97.T8 (ebook) | DDC 326/.8092 [B]—dc23
LC record available at https://lccn.loc.gov/2020005753
LC ebook record available at https://lccn.loc.gov/2020005754

Cherry Lake Publishing Group would like to acknowledge the work of the Partnership for 21st Century Learning, a Network of Battelle for Kids. Please visit http://www.battelleforkids.org/networks/p21 for more information.

Printed in the United States of America
Corporate Graphics

ABOUT THE AUTHOR

Tamra Orr is the author of more than 500 nonfiction books for readers of all ages. A graduate of Ball State University, she now lives in the Pacific Northwest with her family. When she isn't writing books, she is either camping, reading or on the computer researching the latest topics.

TABLE OF CONTENTS

Skipping School

During the 1850s, America was in **turmoil**. The question of civil rights was on everyone's minds. **Abolitionists** fought against slavery. They wrote and gave speeches, protested, and even took up arms during the Civil War. Meanwhile, **suffragists** worked to secure voting rights for women. Often these movements intersected, with many people supporting both. However, the battles for both freedom and universal suffrage were long and difficult.

"Are you sure we should be doing this?" Amos asked his sister as they climbed the long steps of Stone Church in Akron, Ohio. "I mean, if we're going to skip school, shouldn't we be doing something fun, instead of listening to a speech?"

[21ST CENTURY SKILLS LIBRARY]

Sojourner Truth was an important force in combining women's rights with abolition and civil rights.

"Sssssshhh! And no!" replied Tabitha, looking around to see if anyone had overheard Amos. "Didn't you hear Mama and Papa arguing about this **convention** all evening? It lasted from dinnertime until we went to bed. Their voices were so loud. I want to see what they were so heated about."

In the United States, enslaved people were not set free until after the Civil War.

The two of them snuck into the church and took seats in the last row of the crowded, noisy room.

"Don't be ridiculous! You know nothing of which you speak!" an angry man's voice cried out from somewhere in front of them.

"What makes you and me so different? Truly, sir—what?" a woman replied.

[21ST CENTURY SKILLS LIBRARY]

"They sound awfully mad," Amos whispered behind his hand.

"I know," Tabitha agreed, looking around at the audience. It seemed like everyone was upset.

It was the second morning of the Women's Rights Convention on the "Rights, Duties, and Relations of Women." Mama had attended it the first day. That night at dinner, she reported that the speakers read letters and poems aloud, sang songs, and gave reports. Some talked about how the Constitution focused on the importance of equal rights, but only for white men.

"The women at the convention want to change the Constitution to read, 'We hold these truths to be **self-evident**: That all men and women are created equal,'" Mama had explained. Papa had shaken his head and thrown his napkin on the table. "Women need to stay home and focus on supporting their husbands so that they can raise good, moral children," he'd grumbled. Tabitha watched her mother, who sat in silence. She knew that meant Mama was feeling sad.

To escape to freedom, runaway slaves would often have to hide out in the wilderness.

"Uncle Reuben says all these women are just out to stir up trouble," Amos said. "He even said they are going to fight for the right to vote. Can you imagine that? What crazy talk."

Tabitha scowled. "It's not crazy! Mama says these women are fighting for the right to be treated the same as any old man. That includes the right to vote. That seems fair to me!"

[21ST CENTURY SKILLS LIBRARY]

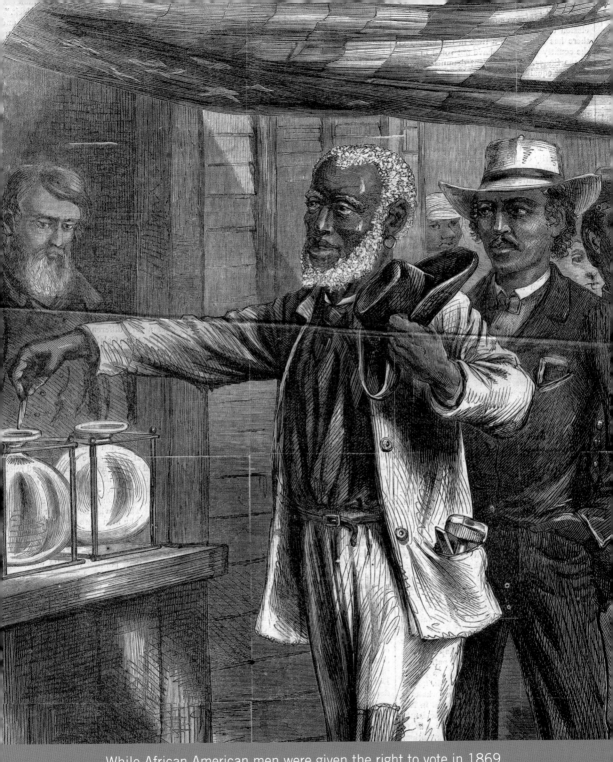

While African American men were given the right to vote in 1869, Southern states found ways to block them from doing so.

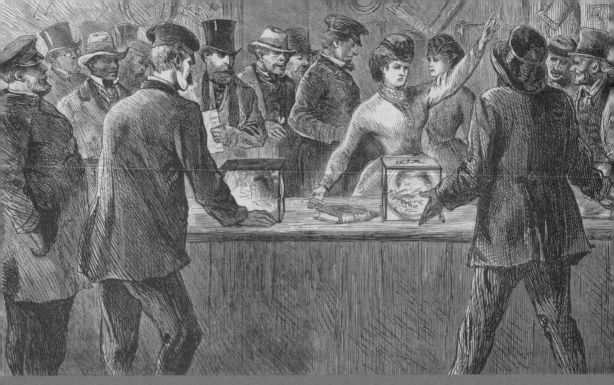

Victoria Woodhull was a prominent suffragist who demanded voting rights. She was also the first woman to run for president.

As time went on, even Tabitha had to admit the meeting was not nearly as exciting as she had imagined. Amos looked like he was about to fall asleep. If this was what the convention was going to be like, they might as well go back to school.

Just then, a man stood up. His face was red. He was clearly angry. "Go home to your husbands and children," he yelled at the speakers onstage. "That's where you belong!"

Another man stood up, nodding his head in agreement. "Women are neither strong enough nor smart enough to vote!" he shouted. The crowd began to talk among themselves.

Amos sat up in his seat, wide awake now. "This is more like it!" he said.

Tabitha glanced around the room. She suspected that the day was going to get more exciting. She just wasn't sure whether or not that was a good thing.

The Rise of Women's Voices

The Women's Rights Convention in Akron, Ohio, in 1851 was not the first time women had spoken out for equality. Three years earlier, in July 1848, a convention was held in Seneca Falls, New York. Suffragist Elizabeth Cady Stanton introduced a document called the Declaration of Rights and Sentiments. Among the rights it outlined was the right to vote. The document received 100 signatures.

A Few Words

At the beginning of the convention, the room had been fairly quiet, but now people were getting upset. The voices of men and women grew loud. Their faces were flushed, and tempers flared.

Suddenly, a tall woman stood up. She had been sitting quietly all morning, but now she turned to the room to speak. She wore small **spectacles**, and her head was in a bright white sunbonnet. She was one of the few African American women in the hall.

"May I say a few words?" she asked, as she began walking to the front of the room. The room buzzed with people mumbling and whispering, but the woman continued walking confidently to the front of the room.

In 1864, Sojourner Truth visited President Abraham Lincoln at the White House.

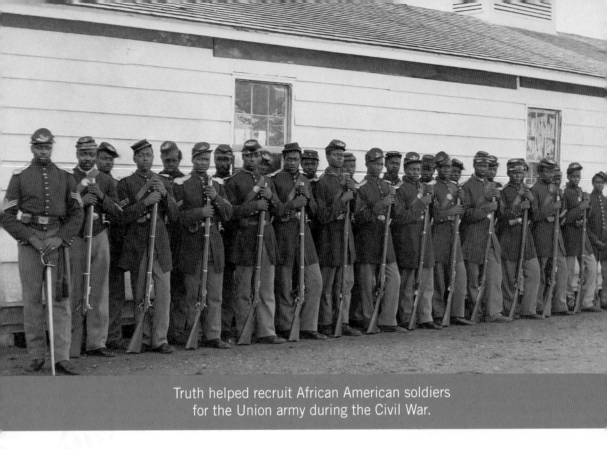

Truth helped recruit African American soldiers
for the Union army during the Civil War.

"Who is she?" Tabitha wondered.

"I think she's one of the freed slaves," Amos replied quietly.
"I heard she might be here. She has been traveling on some kind
of tour in the east. But she's never been as far west as Ohio. She
even wrote a book about her life. She sells it out front."

Tabitha looked at him in surprise. "How do you know all this?"
she asked.

"Uncle Reuben's hotel is the only one in town willing to rent
rooms to the black speakers," Amos said.

Tabitha just stared at him.

Amos blushed. "I've been, well, **eavesdropping** on some of their conversations."

The president of the convention motioned for the woman to come up on the stage. "Ms. Sojourner Truth," she introduced and sat back down.

Truth stood at the **podium**. Her sharp eyes looked at the audience. When she spoke, her deep, rich voice commanded attention.

"I want to say a few words about this matter," she stated. She leaned forward, her voice strong. "I have as much muscle as any man and can do as much work as any man." She pulled up the sleeve of her shirt, showing her arm to the audience as proof.

Amos gasped. It wasn't common for women to show their skin above their elbows. Amos had never even seen his own mother's arms.

Truth traveled and spoke throughout the United States
to fight for an end to slavery.

"I have plowed and reaped and husked and chopped and mowed, and can any man do more than that?" she said. "I can carry as much as any man, and can eat as much too, if I can get it," she continued. "I am as strong as any man that is now."

The crowd broke into whispers.

"See, girls can be just as strong as boys," Tabitha teased, hitting Amos with her elbow.

Amos huffed and shrugged his shoulders in response.

From Isabella to Sojourner

Truth was 54 when she gave her famous speech in Ohio. Born Isabella Baumfree in 1797, she had been bought and sold half a dozen times before she escaped to freedom at the age of 30. After that, she worked as a housekeeper and a cook. In 1843, she changed her name to reflect her new mission in life. It was to travel the world telling people the truth about the hardship that black women faced in the United States. In 1850, she **dictated** *her life story to a writer. She sold copies of her book when she made speeches.*

CHAPTER 3

Standing Tall

Sojourner Truth stood up even taller and told the audience, "You need not be afraid to give us our rights for fear we will take too much. Why children, if you have woman's rights, give it to her and you will feel better."

It was obvious from the chuckles in the room that some people agreed with what she was saying. Other people looked angry. Amos suspected this was not really because of Truth's words. It was probably more because they didn't like a black woman being allowed to speak at all. Truth ended her speech and sat back down.

Truth worked alongside other prominent abolitionists, like Frederick Douglass.

Truth was a deeply spiritual woman. Even though she could not read, she memorized scriptures.

Tabitha had not realized before how many changes these women were hoping to achieve until she listened to Truth's speech. Women wanted equality. Blacks wanted freedom. She tried to imagine what life would be like if either of those things happened.

Soon, the convention **adjourned** for a lunch break. Amos and Tabitha ran outside, eager to move around. As they walked home down High Street, Amos said, "I bet the talk in Uncle Reuben's hotel will be interesting tonight." Tabitha nodded.

For weeks after the convention, everyone was talking about Truth's speech. Many people argued that the changes being proposed were unnecessary. Wasn't life fine just the way it was? Others disagreed. Why shouldn't women be given the same rights as men? Why shouldn't African Americans have the same freedoms? Tabitha's parents often talked long into the evening, and she fell asleep listening to the murmur of their voices.

From One Version to Another

Truth, like many former slaves of her time, could not read or write. She did not write her speeches, but said them as the words came to her. Because of this, there are no written records to prove exactly what she said in any of her speeches. There are two **versions** of what she said in Akron. One was written a few weeks after the convention by reporter Marius Robinson, who was Truth's friend. It was published in Ohio's Anti-Slavery Bugle. The other, which is quoted far more often, was written by Frances Dana Gage and published in the New York Independent a dozen years after the original speech. Gage's version gives Truth a thick Southern accent, which she did not have. It also states that Truth had 13 children, when she actually had five. Gage's version was also much longer than the original speech. It included the famous phrase "Ain't I a woman?" four times. However, it's likely that Truth never actually said those words.

Stirring Up Trouble

"We're here!" Martha yelled as she came through the front door with her two children. She motioned them to the backyard, and the kids raced out back. Martha went in search of her grandmother. She found her sitting at the kitchen table, a newspaper spread out in front of her. To Martha's surprise, there were tears running down her grandmother's face.

"What's wrong? Are you sick?" she asked, rushing over to put her arm around her grandmother's shoulders.

"Look, Martha! It has happened at last." She pointed a trembling finger to the newspaper's headline. "Women Get the Vote!" it stated in huge black letters.

In March 1913, the National American Woman Suffrage Association organized a march in Washington, DC, with more than 5,000 suffragettes.

"Oh, Grandma Tabitha! It has been such a long time coming, hasn't it?" replied Martha.

Just then, Amos, Martha's great-uncle, walked into the kitchen with a big grin on his weathered face. "Finally!" he said, gesturing to the newspaper.

During the 1963 March on Washington, African Americans protested many injustices, including **segregation** in schools.

"Amos, I didn't think we would live to see the day," said Tabitha. "We need to celebrate! Martha, tell the kids I'm making their favorite cookies. Amos, your eyes are better than mine. Read the story to me," she said, as she stood and began gathering ingredients.

Amos read the details of the **amendment** aloud. Tabitha reflected on the long years that had passed since she and her brother had heard Sojourner Truth's speech. Neither one of them could have imagined that women would have had to work this long and hard to get equal rights.

African American women contributed to the war effort during World War II
but still lived segregated lives in the South.

Today's movements focus on achieving justice and equality
for everyone regardless of race or gender.

"I am so glad we are here to see these changes in our country," said Tabitha as she broke eggs into a mixing bowl.

"Me too," agreed Amos. He couldn't help adding, "It's amazing what can happen when women decide to 'stir up trouble.'"

Just as he expected, Tabitha showed him her familiar scowl.

A Long Time Coming

The passage of the 15th and 19th Amendments were widely celebrated as victories. But African American women still found themselves left out. They had fought alongside both African American men and white women for universal suffrage and freedoms. But the 15th Amendment granted only African American men the right to vote, and the 19th Amendment solely benefited white women. Black women were often not given the credit they deserved. As it would turn out, many obstacles would continue to prevent people of color from exercising their right to vote—until 1965. That year, the Voting Rights Act was passed. The act banned racial **discrimination** in voting practices. This was the moment civil rights leaders had worked hard for. Even today, though, the fight is not over. People of color still find themselves battling discrimination and injustice from governments and organizations.

1851

Truth speaks at the Women's Rights Convention in Akron, Ohio.

1843

Truth changes her name to reflect her new mission in life.

1845

1830

1827

Sojourner Truth escapes to freedom.

1850

Truth dictates her autobiography, *The Narrative of Sojourner Truth.*

1883
Truth dies at age 86.

1865
The Civil War ends in April. By December, the 13th Amendment is passed, ending slavery.

1860

1875

1869
The 15th Amendment is passed, allowing black men to vote.

1861
The Civil War begins.

Speech Highlight

"*May I say a few words? I want to say a few words about this matter. I am a woman's rights. I have as much muscle as any man, and can do as much work as any man. I have plowed and reaped and husked and chopped and mowed, and can any man do more than that? I have heard much about the sexes being equal; I can carry as much as any man, and can eat as much too, if I can get it. I am as strong as any man that is now. As for intellect, all I can say is, if women have a pint and man a quart—why can't she have her little pint full? You need not be afraid to give us our rights for fear we will take too much, for we can't take more than our pint'll hold.*"

Read the full speech at https://www.thesojournertruthproject.com/compare-the-speeches.

Research and Act

Sojourner Truth's message was that women are just as strong, capable, and intelligent as men are, so they deserve equal rights. Almost 170 years after her speech, the nation still struggles with issues of equal rights.

Research

Do some reading about an issue you see happening today where people are not necessarily given the same rights. Read about it and why it is happening. What are people's thoughts on each side of the problem?

Act

Think about what Sojourner Truth would have said about the issue you've been researching. Write a two-paragraph speech from her perspective, based on what you have learned about her activism.

Further Reading

McDonough, Yona Zeldis. *Who Was Sojourner Truth?* New York, NY: Grosset and Dunlap, 2015.

Schmidt, Gary. *So Tall Within: Sojourner Truth's Long Walk Toward Freedom.* New York, NY: Roaring Brook Press, 2018.

Taylor, Charlotte. *Sojourner Truth: Abolitionist and Activist.* New York, NY: Enslow Publishing, 2016.

Turner, Ann. *My Name Is Truth: The Life of Sojourner Truth.* New York, NY: Harper, 2015.

GLOSSARY

abolitionists (ab-uh-LISH-uh-nists) people who worked to put an end to slavery

adjourned (uh-JURND) to close or end something, such as a meeting

amendment (uh-MEND-muhnt) a change made to a law or legal document, such as the U.S. Constitution

convention (kuhn-VEN-shuhn) the gathering of people for a common purpose

dictated (DIK-tay-tid) speaking words out loud so they can be written down

discrimination (dis-krim-uh-NAY-shuhn) unfair treatment of someone based on differences in such things as race or gender

eavesdropping (EEVZ-drahp-ing) listening to a conversation secretly

podium (POH-dee-uhm) a stand with a surface for holding papers, for use by a person giving a speech

segregation (seg-rih-GAY-shuhn) the practice of keeping people or groups apart

self-evident (self-EV-ih-duhnt) clear; not needing proof

spectacles (SPEK-tuh-kuhlz) eyeglasses

suffragists (SUHF-rij-ists) people who worked to get women the right to vote

turmoil (TUR-moil) a state of great confusion

versions (VUR-zhuhns) accounts of an event from specific points of view

INDEX